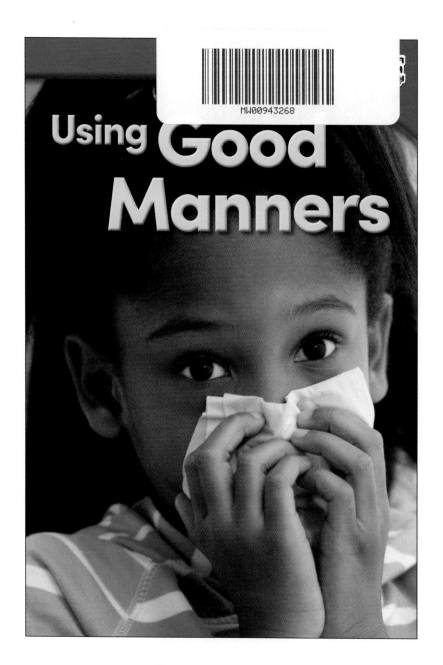

Using Good Manners

Sharon Coan

Publishing Credits

Rachelle Cracchiolo, M.S.Ed., *Publisher*
Conni Medina, M.A.Ed., *Managing Editor*
Jamey Acosta, *Content Director*
Dona Herweck Rice, *Series Developer*
Robin Erickson, *Multimedia Designer*

Image Credits: p.3 ©iStock.com/Chris Bernard Photography, Inc.; pp.4, Back Cover ©iStock.com/RapidEye; pp.6, 12 ©iStock.com/betoon; p.10 ©Image Source Plus/Alamy; p.11 ©iStock.com/Pamela Moore; all other images from Shutterstock.

Library of Congress Cataloging-in-Publication Data

Library of Congress Control Number: 2015938710

Teacher Created Materials

5301 Oceanus Drive
Huntington Beach, CA 92649-1030
http://www.tcmpub.com

ISBN 978-1-4938-2064-1

© 2016 Teacher Created Materials, Inc.
Printed in China
Nordica.082019.CA21901094

good

bad

good

bad

good

bad

good

bad

good

Words to Know

bad

good